Comebacks for Lawyer Jokes

The Restatement of Retorts

Written and compiled by

Malcolm Kushner, AFHC

Museum of Humor.com Press

Table of Contents

Introduction

Lawyer jokes have probably been around since cave-men stopped using clubs for dispute resolution and started suing their neighbors instead. Unfortunately, the stereotype perpetuated by these jokes isn't pretty. Lawyers are portrayed as rich, greedy, pompous, boring and narcissistic, among other negative traits. Death and taxes are supposed to be the only things certain in the world. But you can add lawyer jokes to the list. Throughout history, such jokes have periodically appeared in many countries around the globe.

As early as ancient Greek times, the playwright Aristophanes satirized sophists. Forerunners of lawyers, sophists were experts on persuasion who taught citizens how to argue—especially legal cases. Aristophanes ridiculed them extensively in his classic play *The Clouds*.

Jumping ahead, to approximately 1591, we arrive at another famous play—Shakespeare's *Henry the VI, Part II*. It includes the line that has become the bane of attorneys ever since: "The first thing we do, let's kill all the lawyers." The meaning of the line has been argued about endlessly. But it was definitely designed to get a laugh from the audience. And it still does.

While these comic jibes are clearly directed at legal practitioners, they're not really jokes in the traditional sense of the word. That changed in 1739 with the publication of a book known as *Joe Miller's Jests*. It was a compendium of jokes that included the following:

A worthy old Gentleman in the Country, having employ'd an Attorney, of whom he had a pretty good Opinion, to do some Law Business for him in *London*, he was greatly surprized on his coming to Town, and demanding his Bill of Law Charges, to find that it amounted to at least three Times the Sum he expected; the honest Attorney assured him, that there was no Article in his Bill, but what was *fair and reasonable:* Nay, said the Country Gentleman, here is one of them I am sure cannot be so, for you have set down three Shillings and four Pence for going to *Southwark*, when none of my Business lay that Way; pray what is the Meaning of that Sir; *Oh! Sir*, said he, *that was for fetching the* Chine *and* Turkey *from the Carriers, that you sent me for a* Present, *out of the Country.*

An edition published in 1836 also included:

A knavish attorney asking a very worthy gentleman, what was honesty? What is that to you? said he; meddle with those things that concern you.

A farm was lately advertised in a newspaper in which all the beauty of the situation, fertility of the soil, and salubrity of the air, were detailed in the richest glow of rural description, and which was further enhanced with this N.B. There is not an attorney within fifteen miles of the neighbourhood.

Hey, those sound like lawyer jokes to me!

Fast forward to the 20th century. While lawyer jokes had always been around, they became especially prevalent between 1950 and 2000. Marc Galanter, a distinguished law professor, sociologist and authority on the history of lawyer jokes, attributes this to the expansion of law in America throughout the 1950s, 60s and 70s. He also notes that the jokes became more frequent and hostile in the 1980s.

What caused this change? We can speculate forever: an ever-increasing number of lawyers moving into the workforce; a profusion of seemingly frivolous litigation; an explosion of legal advertising; the fact that I became a lawyer in 1980.

Whatever the reason, the early 1980s produced an exceedingly large number of lawyer jokes. You know what I'm talking about—skid marks, professional courtesy, not enough cement. The list goes on. It got so bad that a frustrated state bar leader advised lawyers to launch preemptive attacks by telling doctor jokes. (My favorite: What do you call a surgeon who wears a suit? The defendant.) The strategy did not prove successful. But the jokes did eventually diminish for awhile. That's because all joke cycles ebb and flow; and by the end of the 1980s lawyer jokes were definitely ebbing.

Unfortunately, the reprieve was short-lived. By the early 1990s, lawyer humor had returned and probably peaked in 1993. That's when audiences laughed out loud when a lawyer got eaten by a dinosaur in the *Jurassic Park* movie and a rodeo cowboy lassoed a lawyer in a Miller Lite television commercial. So of course lawyer jokes were back in force. But it was an especially tragic event that made 1993 an iconic year for lawyer humor.

On July 1, 1993, a disgruntled businessman invaded the office of a San Francisco law firm and shot and killed eight people including three lawyers. Subsequently Harvey Saferstein, then the president of the California bar, linked the killings to lawyer jokes. He likened the jokes to hate speech and suggested that anyone telling them should receive special penalties. The response was immediate, negative and opened the floodgates for even more lawyer-bashing humor. Here are two examples.

Paul Conrad, the cartoonist for *The Los Angeles Times*, depicted the bar president as a clown. "The latest lawyer joke, Harvey Saferstein," the caption read. Rob Morse, of *The San Francisco Examiner*, called Mr. Saferstein's campaign "grotesque." "Protect lawyers as a special class of people?" he asked. "It's hard to believe lawyers are more endangered than 7-Eleven clerks."

In a letter to *The Times*, Robert Pugsley, who teaches criminal law and legal ethics at the Southwestern University School of Law in Los Angeles, contended that labeling lawyer-bashing as hate speech and punishing perpetrators would trample on the Constitution. "Watch out, Jay Leno," he wrote. "Goodbye, First Amendment."

–David Margolick writing in
The New York Times, July 9, 1993

Imagine that: Lawyer wants to classify anti-attorney speech—known to laypeople as jokes—as criminal. Hey, why should a lawyer care about constitutional protections, about free speech? We're talking hurt feelings here.

Can't you just see the public-service announcements: Dis an attorney, go to jail.

The possibilities boggle the mind: You are charged with asking why lawyers don't go to the beach. In a tense courtroom moment, you confess: "Yes, your honor, I told the joke. The reason lawyers do not go to the beach is because cats keep trying to bury them."

–Robin Abcarian writing in
The Los Angeles Times, July 11, 1993

You get the idea. Eventually the uproar petered out and the jokes resumed their normal cycle, spiking again in the early 2000s.

Lawyer jokes are an international phenomenon. A quick Google search reveals that, in addition to the United States, they're prevalent in the United Kingdom, Australia, India and many other countries. (Search for "solicitor jokes.") In fact a headline from Canada's leading newspaper, *The Globe and Mail*, illustrates the international nature of the problem: "Tired of being the butt of jokes, Ontario lawyers plan image overhaul." The story, which ran on February 6, 2013, described a public relations campaign funded by the Ontario Bar Association to persuade people that real lawyers are not the stereotypes conveyed in lawyer jokes.

So the earth goes around the sun, the world turns, and the lawyer jokes continue to flow endlessly. That's why I've written this book. It's designed to help lawyers cope with the inevitable jokes, the ones you'll be told as soon as someone learns that you're a member of the bar.

The book is divided into three parts conveniently labeled Part I, Part II and Part III.

Part I: Defense Without Being Defensive offers comebacks to a wide variety of popular lawyer jokes. The comebacks function as alternative punch-lines that allow you to break the normal pattern of the jokes and turn the tables on the joke teller. They should be used as your first line of defense against the boors who tell lawyer jokes.

Part II: Offense consists of jokes about doctors, CPAs and other professionals who often tell lawyer jokes. These are for use when the comebacks in Part I don't silence the miscreant telling the jokes. The jokes in this part enable you to escalate the confrontation and go on the attack.

Part III: Jokes That Make Lawyers Look Good contains jokes that promote a positive image of attorneys.

You should tell them wherever, whenever and to whomever you can.

It is my sincere hope that the tools in this book will provide a useful shield, and occasional sword, in your battle with lawyer jokes. Use them wisely. And that's no joke!

Part I

Defense Without Being Defensive

You're at a party. You mention you're a lawyer. And the jokes start coming fast and furious: snakes, professional courtesy, skid marks, death. If you object, you have no sense of humor. If you smile and take it—well no one, especially lawyers, wants to smile and take it. So what do you do?

"The best defense is a good offense." These words of wisdom are often treated as gospel in sports, politics, military and other competitive endeavors. Why? According to Wikipedia, "the idea is that strong offensive action will preoccupy the opposition and ultimately hinder its ability to mount an opposing counterattack, leading to a strategic advantage."

So in an adversarial arena like the law, it's natural that many attorneys believe the best defense is a good offense. But is it really? Not for dealing with lawyer jokes in a social situation.

Here's why.

Under the best defense is a good offense doctrine, you must *initiate* the attack. While this might be a good strategy in litigation, being the aggressor in a social conversation is not. Why? Let's say you're at a party or other social setting. Before anyone can tell a lawyer joke, you tell a joke about their profession. What's the reaction? You'll be viewed as a jerk. You'll just re-enforce the stereotype that lawyers are mean, hostile, aggressive and full of themselves. So you can't strike first.

That's why I believe the best strategy is a *great defense*. And that's what this part of the book is all about.

You *don't* have to take it when someone tells a lawyer joke. But the key to success is your *response* to the joke—the clever comeback, the witty retort. Your response should silence the joke teller. And it's not that difficult to do. Because even though your audience may not be sympathetic to lawyers, it will recognize that you were attacked first. So when you unleash your jibe back, the audience will have some motivation to be on your side. They'll laugh *with* you and *at* the joke teller.

Now I know what you're thinking. My analysis makes perfect sense, but it neglects a crucial issue. What exactly do you say? How do you instantly come up with a stingingly witty retort that shuts down the person telling lawyer jokes? That's the crux of the matter.

And the truth is most people—even lawyers—can't come up with a brilliant response on the spur of the moment. Once in awhile you'll run into someone who can. But they are rare indeed. If you think of a response at all, it's usually days, weeks or months later—far too late to be of any use. So what are you, as the victim of a lawyer joke, to do?

The answer is surprisingly simple: anticipate and prepare. And your legal training has already enabled you to master these techniques.

Attorneys routinely anticipate objections, tough questions, deal breakers and other problems. Good attorneys are prepared for them. The same process applies to dealing with insulting questions posing as humor. You anticipate what the boor will say and you have a line ready to respond.

A quick web-search reveals that many people have already created sites with responses to annoying questions about specific personal or professional issues. A perfect example is "Women's Responses to Men's Pick-up Lines." Here's a sample:

Q: What would it take to get you to leave
   here with me?
A: A fire.

And that just scratches the surface. A wide variety of groups have anticipated common awkward or embarrassing questions and posted comebacks to them on web pages all across the internet. Here are some examples.

For Vegetarians

Q: Isn't vegetarianism weird?
A: Not quite as weird as killing animals
   and burying their remains in your body.

For Singles

Q: Why aren't you married yet?
A: Just lucky, I guess.

For Magicians

Q: Can you make my wife disappear?
A: I could, but who would hand you the remote?"

For Artists

Q: Can you give me a freebie? It'll be great exposure.
A: Drop trou. It'll be great exposure.

And you can find a lot more by googling "witty retorts" or "witty comebacks" or similar search terms.

Surprisingly, one group that has not embraced this method is attorneys. You'd think that professionals known for their command of words who claim to loathe lawyer jokes would have created numerous pages of responses to spring on their antagonists. But months of web research has not revealed any. (More research might be needed, but my wife told me to get a life.)

In order to rectify this dearth of retorts, I've written the first part of this book. It includes comebacks for some of the most annoying jokes commonly directed at attorneys. The comebacks basically function as alternative punch-lines. When people ask the question that sets up the joke, you respond with the comeback before they can say the traditional punch-line. That gets everyone laughing *with* you and *at* the jerks who tell lawyer jokes.

How many lawyer jokes are there?

Hundreds—but they're all serving in Congress.

Only three. The rest are true stories.

What's black and brown and looks really good on a lawyer?

A pair of boots.

A Doberman Pinscher.

Why is it so hard to drown a lawyer?

You say

Their clients think they walk on water.

Before they say

Pond scum floats.

What's the difference between an accountant and a lawyer?

You say

80 points on the LSAT.

Before they say

Accountants know
they're boring.

What do you call 25 skydiving lawyers?

Down to earth.

Skeet.

Why did the post office recall the new lawyer stamps?

You say

They'd only stick to the
letter of the law.

Before they say

Because people could not
tell which side to spit on.

You are stuck in an elevator with a tiger, a lion and a lawyer. You have a gun with just two bullets in it.
What do you do?

Shoot the lion and tiger.
And hire the lawyer to sue
the building owner.

Shoot the lawyer twice.

What's the difference between a mosquito and a lawyer?

No one ever got malaria
from a lawyer.*

One is a blood-sucking
parasite, the other is
an insect.

*Written by Bob Mills

Why won't sharks attack lawyers?

You say

They need them to negotiate contracts for the Discovery Channel's annual "Shark Week."

Before they say

Professional courtesy.

What do you call 25 lawyers buried up to their necks in sand?

You say

The bar association's family day at the beach.

Before they say

Not enough sand.

Why are lawyers like laxatives?

You say

They both make everything
come out all right.

Before they say

They irritate the crap out
of you.

How are an apple and a lawyer alike?

They both keep the doctor away.

They both look good hanging from a tree.

What's the difference between a lawyer and a trampoline?

You say

A trampoline can't spring to your defense.

Before they say

You take off your shoes before you jump on a trampoline.

What do mold, ooze, pond scum and lawyers have in common?

You say

> They all float to the top.

Before they say

> They're all slime.

What's the difference between a lawyer and a rooster?

You say

> If roosters lose a case, they crow. If lawyers lose a case, they eat crow.

Before they say

> When a rooster wakes up in the morning, its primal urge is to cluck defiance.

Why are lawyers so good at racquetball?

They know their way around a court.

Because they stoop so low.

What's the difference between a lawyer and a leech?

No one wants a lawyer
who sucks.

After you die, a leech stops
sucking your blood.

Why is that so many lawyers have broken noses?

You say

> Clients don't want them
> to take it on the chin.

Before they say

> From chasing parked
> ambulances.

What do beavers and lawyers have in common?

They're both busy and give a dam about their work.

They both get in the mainstream and dam it up.

What would happen if you lock a zombie in a roomful of lawyers?

You say

> They'd advise against
> a living will.

Before they say

> He'd starve to death.

What is the lawyer's creed?

You say

I came. I saw. I argued.

Before they say

The client is innocent until proven broke.

What's the difference between a lawyer and a catfish?

You say

You never let a lawyer off the hook.

Before they say

One is a cold-blooded, bottom-dwelling, scum-sucking scavenger. The other is a fish.

Why did the lawyer go to heaven?

He wanted to live in a gated community.

Hell was full.

Why don't lawyers go to the beach?

You say

They like to avoid flip flops.

Before they say

Cats keep trying to bury them.

Why are there so many lawyers?

You say

They have good breeding.

Before they say

No one would stand in line
to see one.

Why is going to a meeting of the Bar Association like going into a bait shop?

Everyone is saying the settlement they negotiated was "this big" [spread hands apart].

Because of the abundance of suckers, leeches, maggots and night crawlers.

What's the difference between an honest lawyer and a solar eclipse?

You say

An honest lawyer doesn't cast a shadow over your case.

Before they say

You can see a solar eclipse every seventy-five years.

What do you get when you cross a pitbull with a lawyer?

You say

> A lawyer that will sink his teeth into your case.

Before they say

> A dishonest pitbull.

Have you heard about the lawyers' word processor?

You say

Word processor—that's Latin for secretary.

Before they say

No matter what font you select, everything comes out in fine print.

How can you tell if a lawyer is well hung?

You say

> He screws the opposition and they ask for more.

Before they say

> You can't get a finger between the rope and his neck.

What's the difference between a porcupine and a Mercedes Benz full of lawyers?

You say

Quills vs. bills.

Before they say

The porcupine has pricks
on the outside.

Did you hear about the new parachutes designed especially for lawyers?

You say

They're all golden.

Before they say

They open automatically on impact.

What do you get when you cross a pig with a lawyer?

Someone who even defends a squealer.

Nothing. There are some things that even a pig won't do.

What does pond scum have more of than lawyers?

You say

Slime.

Before they say

Respect.

What's the difference between a lawyer and an onion?

Lawyers don't have thin skins.

No one cries when they cut up a lawyer.

What's the difference between an orthodontist and a lawyer?

You say

> Once encases your face with braces; the other braces to face your cases.

Before they say

> You get your money's worth from the orthodontist's retainer.

What's the difference between a lawyer and a prostitute?

They're both professions, but only one is the world's oldest.

A prostitute will stop screwing you when you're dead.

Why are lawyers great in bed?

You say

> They won't roll over on you.

Before they say

> They get so much practice
> screwing people.

What's the difference between an amoeba and a lawyer?

One is a cell; the other keeps you out of a cell.

One wears a tie.

What do you get when you cross the Godfather with a lawyer?

You say

A *very* final contract.

Before they say

An offer you can't understand.

How many lawyers does it take to paint a wall?

Two. One to get the paint
and one to get it in the lease.

It depends how hard you
throw them.

What do dinosaurs and decent lawyers have in common?

You say

Thick skins.

Before they say

They're both extinct.

What do lawyers do after they die?

Avoid probate.

They lie still.

What's the difference between a lawyer and a liar?

A polygraph test.

The pronunciation.

What's the difference between a law firm and a circus?

You say

One has a lion tamer, the other a lien tamer.

Before they say

At a circus, the clowns don't charge the public by the hour.

How do you get a lawyer out of a tree?

You say

> Very carefully.

Before they say

> Cut the rope.

What is the difference between a jellyfish and a lawyer?

Aquariums don't beg
jellyfish to be on their
board of directors.

One's a spineless, poisonous
blob. The other is a form
of sea life.

What do you call a lawyer in handcuffs?

You say

Kinky.

Before they say

Trustworthy.

What's a good wedding present for a lawyer who marries another lawyer?

You say

A matching set of prenups.

Before they say

Towels marked Hiss and Hiss.

How many lawyers does it take to change a light bulb?

None. That's a job for a paralegal.

Three. One to climb the ladder. One to shake it. And one to sue the ladder company.

What can a goose do, a duck can't and a lawyer should?

You say

Lay a golden egg.

Before they say

Stick his bill up his ass.

What do you get when you cross one lawyer with another lawyer?

An attorney who responds on the double.

Nothing. There are some things that not even nature can permit.

Why are lawyers like nuclear weapons?

They both radiate warmth.

If one side has one, the other side has to get one. Once launched, they cannot be recalled. When they land, they screw up everything forever.

What's the difference between a good lawyer and a bad lawyer?

You say

A bad lawyer bails on you.
A good lawyer gets you bail.

Before they say

A bad lawyer makes your case drag on for years.
A good lawyer makes it last even longer.

Why don't lawyers play golf?

They already work with enough people who are tee'd off.

Too much like work with all of the lying involved.

What's the difference between a lawyer and a plumber?

When they accept your case,
lawyers take a plunge and
plumbers take a plunger

A plumber works to unclog
the system.

What's the difference between a lawyer and a vampire?

You say

Vampires only go to night court.

Before they say

A vampire only sucks blood at night.

What do a baker and an attorney have in common?

You say

They both have clients who take the cake.

Before they say

They both enjoy carving up the pie.

What's the difference between pigs and lawyers?

You say

One brings home the bacon;
the other is the bacon.

Before they say

You can learn to respect
a pig.

Why do they bury lawyers under 20 feet of dirt?

You say

So they can't think outside
the box.

Before they say

Because deep down,
they're really good people.

What happened to the banker who went to law school?

Now her interest in justice
is compounded daily.

Now she's a loan shark.

Where do vampires learn to suck blood?

Medical school: when they run out of leeches.

Law school.

What's the difference between a brilliant lawyer and a stupid lawyer?

Jail time.

Brilliance has its limits.

Why don't lawyers play hide-and-seek?

You say

It violates Discovery rules.

Before they say

Nobody will look for them.

What does it mean when a lawyer tells his clients he has a sliding fee schedule?

You say

It means he has a second job playing trombone.

Before they say

It means that after you pay his bill, it's financially hard to get back on your feet.

How many lawyers can you place on the point of a needle?

You say

> Enough to sew up a case.

Before they say

> Ten, if you stand them on their heads.

What's the first thing you should do after running over a lawyer?

Call a different lawyer.

Back up.

What's the difference between a poisonous snake and a lawyer?

A lawyer saves his venom
for the courtroom.

You can make a pet out
of the snake.

What's the difference between a vacuum cleaner and a lawyer on a motorcycle?

You say

A lawyer on a motorcycle sucks only if he loses your case; a vacuum cleaner just sucks.

Before they say

The vacuum cleaner has the dirt bag on the inside.

What's the difference between a lawyer and a pothole?

A lawyer has more depth.

None, except that nobody runs over the same pothole twice.

What's the difference between a flea and a lawyer?

A lawyer doesn't want to be on a case that's a dog.

One is a parasite that sucks the living blood out of you and is linked with the Black Death. The other is a small insect.

What's the difference between a lawyer and an undertaker?

A lawyer doesn't mind getting buried in his work.

A lawyer doesn't mind getting his hands dirty while burying his victims.

What's the difference between a lawyer and a boxing referee?

A lawyer always wins
by a decision.

A boxing referee doesn't get
paid more for a longer fight.

What does a lawyer get when you give him Viagra?

You say

An extension for your case.

Before they say

Taller.

What's the difference between a lawyer and a Dalmatian?

You say

A Dalmatian can't connect the dots.

Before they say

A Dalmatian knows when to stop chasing the ambulance.

How do you spot an honest lawyer?

He gives you his irrevocable trust.

No one knows.

Do you know why being a lawyer is the opposite of having sex?

You say

You *start* when someone has a headache.

Before they say

Because it's all bad and some is worse.

How do you stop a lawyer from drowning?

You say

> With an argument that holds water.

Before they say

> Shoot him before he hits the water.

What's the difference between a dry cleaner and a lawyer?

You say

One takes your suit and makes it look as good as possible. The other is a dry cleaner.

Before they say

The cleaner pays you if he loses your suit. If a lawyer loses your suit, he will still take you to the cleaners.

What's the best thing to give a lawyer in the hospital?

> Blanket coverage.

> A nurse who believes in euthanasia.

What's the difference between a stagecoach and a lawyer?

> One likes happy trails;
> the other, happy trials.

> One is built for the long haul
> and runs roughshod over
> everything in its path;
> the other carries passengers.

What do lawyers and bullfrogs have in common?

You say

People get upset if they croak.

Before they say

Both have a big head that consists mostly of mouth.

What's the difference between a lawyer and an angry rhinoceros?

You say

The lawyer charges with a credit card.

Before they say

The lawyer charges more.

What's the difference between a lawyer and a bag of fertilizer?

You say

You never want your lawyer spread too thin.

Before they say

One's a bag of crap, and the other's fertilizer.

Why don't lawyers fall in love on Valentine's Day?

You say

Cupid can't get a bow and arrow into a courtroom.

Before they say

Oh, come on. Even Cupid can't hit a target that small.

What's the difference between a stork and an attorney?

Gangsters in old movies never go to the "Attorney Club".

One can stick its bill up its ass; the other one should.

What's the difference between a lawyer and God?

You say

During sex nobody yells "Oh lawyer".

Before they say

God doesn't think He's a lawyer.

Santa Claus, the Tooth Fairy, an honest lawyer and a drunk are in a bar when they spot a hundred dollars on the floor. Who gets it?

The waitress.

The drunk—the other three are mythological characters.

Why did the lawyer cross the road?

To negotiate with the
other side.

To get to the accident on
the other side.

What's the difference between baseball and the law?

> Lawyer cards don't come
> with gum.

> In baseball, if you're caught
> stealing, you're out.

What do lawyers use for birth control?

Condom-nation procedures.

Their personalities.

What's the difference between a lawyer and a gigolo?

A hung jury vs. a well hung jury.

A gigolo only screws one person at a time.

What's the difference between a lawyer and a skunk?

You say

With a lawyer, nothing is ever black and white.

Before they say

Nobody wants to hit a skunk.

How do you kill a trial lawyer when he's drinking?

You say

> Give him the burden
> of 100 proof.

Before they say

> Slam the toilet seat on
> his head.

What's the difference between a lawyer and a football?

One is inflated with air, controlled by the clock and scores points against the other side. The other is a football.

You only get three points for kicking a football between the uprights.

What do lawyers and prostitutes have in common?

You say

Billable hours.

Before they say

If you pay them, they will screw you.

What do you call a criminal lawyer?

An oxymoron. It's like saying "an exact estimate" or "a working vacation".

Redundant.

Why are lawyers being used in research instead of lab rats?

You say

They're smart, disciplined and can quickly get through a maze.

Before they say

Three reasons:
1. There are more lawyers than rats.
2. The researchers don't get attached to them.
3. There are some things a rat won't do.

What do you buy a friend graduating from law school?

You say

A book of comebacks to lawyer jokes.

Before they say

A lobotomy.

Why did God invent lawyers?

To defend medical
malpractice cases.

So real estate agents would
have someone to look up to.

What do a lawyer and a sperm have in common?

They work their tails off.

They both hope to become human someday.

What's the difference between a cat and a lawyer?

You say

> More people are allergic
> to cats.

Before they say

> One is an arrogant creature
> that will claw you out of
> house and money, and the
> other is a cat.

How does an attorney sleep?

On *your* side

First he lies on one side;
then he lies on the other.

If you laid all the lawyers in the world end to end, how far would they reach?

To a higher court.

Into the pocket of the next one.

What's the difference between a lawyer and a bucket of manure?

You say

One is full of crap and the other is a lawyer.

Before they say

The bucket.

How can a pregnant woman tell that she's carrying a future lawyer?

> She keeps telling everyone her due process date.

> She has an uncontrollable craving for baloney.

What do you get when you cross a librarian with a lawyer?

Someone everyone wants
to check out.

All the information you
need—but you can't
understand a word of it.

Why are there so many lawyers in the United States?

You say

> The U.S. had first choice.

Before they say

> Because St. Patrick chased the snakes out of Ireland.

Did you hear about the lawyer who stepped in cow dung?

He was brilliant even when the chips were down.

He thought he melted.

What do you call 5000 dead lawyers at the bottom of the ocean?

The Bar Association
of Atlantis.

A good start.

How many law professors does it take to change a light bulb?

You say

None. That's a job for a research assistant.

Before they say

Hell, you need 250 just to lobby for the research grant.

What's the problem with lawyer jokes?

The punchlines need to be doctored.

Lawyers don't think they're funny and no one else thinks they're jokes.

Part II

Offense

Some people just don't know when to stop. They're oblivious to social cues. They can't take a hint. And they haven't got a clue. Unsurprisingly, they're often the people who tell lawyer jokes—even after you've used the comebacks from the first part of this book.

So how do you shut them up?

You've tried to be nice. You've tried to deflect the jokes with alternate punch-lines. But that hasn't worked. So it's time to go on the offensive. Stronger measures are now appropriate.

In this part of the book, you will find jokes about doctors, CPAs and other professionals who like to tell lawyer jokes. They seem to share a lot of the same traits as the lawyers portrayed in those jokes. They come across as greedy, shady, narcissistic, and boring.

Basically, they're jerks—just like the people telling you lawyer jokes.

But still, is it really OK to tell jokes about them? Must you stoop to their level? Shouldn't you turn the other cheek?

That's up to you. But if people wouldn't stop telling lawyer jokes after several polite attempts to stop them, I'd only turn the other cheek to say kiss my butt. And, effectively, that's what these jokes are telling them. Hey, they've asked for it!

Jokes About CPAs

Q: Why did the CPA cross the road?
A: To bore the people on the other side.

Q: What's an extroverted accountant?
A: One who looks at your shoes while he's talking to you instead of his own.

Q: When does a person decide to become an accountant?
A: When he realizes he doesn't have the charisma to succeed as an undertaker.

Q: What do you call an accountant who marries an actuary?
A: A social climber.

Q: If an accountant's wife can't get to sleep, what does she say?
A: "Tell me about work today, dear."

Q: What did the tax accountant do to liven up the office party?

A: Not show up.

Q: What's the definition of an accountant?

A: Someone who solves a problem you didn't know you had in a way you don't understand.

Q: What do you call an accountant without a spreadsheet?

A: Lost.

Q: Why don't accountants stare out of their office windows during the morning?

A: Because they'd have nothing to do at lunchtime.

Q: How does an accountant make a bold fashion statement?

A: He wears his gray suit instead of the blue.

Q: Why do accountants get excited on Saturdays?

A: They can wear casual clothes to work.

Q: How do you know when an accountant's on vacation?

A: He doesn't wear a tie to work and comes in after 8:30.

Q: How many accountants does it take to find a $1.00 mistake in an expense report?

A: Three. One to find the mistake and two to discuss the significance of it.

Q: What's an actuary?

A: An accountant without the sense of humor.

Q: What do actuaries do to liven up their office party?

A: Invite an accountant.

Q: Why did God create economists?

A: So CPAs would have someone to laugh at!

Q: What's an auditor?

A: Someone who arrives after the battle and bayonets all the wounded.

Q: How can you tell when the chief accountant is getting soft?
A: When he actually listens to marketing before saying "No."

Q: How many accountants does it take to change a light bulb?
A: Hmmm . . . I'll just do a few numbers and get back to you.

Q: What do CPAs miss most about a great party?
A: The invitation.

Q: Why did the CPA cross the road?
A: Because that's what he did last year.

Q: Why did he cross back?
A: So he could charge the client for travel expenses.

Q: What's the difference between the short and long income tax forms?
A: If you use the short form, the government gets your money. If you use the long form, the CPA gets your money.

Q: Did you hear about the new microwave CPA?
A: He can cook your books in under a minute.

Q: When do accountants laugh out loud?
A: When somebody asks for a raise.

Q: What's an accountant's idea of trashing his hotel room?
A: Refusing to fill out the guest comment card.

Q: How many accountants does it take to change a light bulb?
A: Two. One to change the bulb and one to check it was done within budget.

Q: What do CPAs do?
A: They put the numb in numbers.

Jokes About Doctors

Q: Why do only 10% of doctors go to heaven?
A: Because if all of them went it would be hell.

Q: Why are jokes about lawyers always one-liners?
A: So doctors can understand them.

Q: What are the three longest years of an orthopedic surgeon's training?
A: First grade.

Q: What is the difference between God and an orthopedic surgeon?
A: God doesn't think He is an orthopedic surgeon.

Q: Did you hear about the little boy who played doctor with the little girl?
A: He made her wait 45 minutes and then double-billed the insurance company.

Q: What do you call two orthopedic surgeons reading a chest x-ray?
A: A double blind study.

Q. What accounts for the largest portion of health care costs?

A. Doctors trying to recoup their investment losses.

Q: What's the difference between a carpenter and an orthopedic surgeon?

A: A carpenter knows more than one antibiotic.

Q: What's the difference between a general practitioner and a specialist?

A: One treats what you have; the other thinks you have what he treats.

Q: What do you call a surgeon in a three-piece suit?

A: The defendant.

Q: What is 12 inches long and hangs in front of an asshole?

A: A stethoscope.

Q. Did you hear about the nurse who died and went straight to hell?

A: It took her two weeks to realize that she wasn't at work anymore!

Q: What's the difference between a nurse and a nun?

A: A nun only has to worship one god.

Q: An internist, a radiologist, a good orthopedist and a bad orthopedist stand in the four corners of a football field. In the center is a pot with $10,000. Who gets the money?

A: The bad orthopedist. The internist will first meditate about the possible ways to get there, the radiologist won't lift a finger for such little money, and there's no such thing as a good orthopedist.

Q: What's the difference between a medical director and a toilet?

A: A toilet only has to deal with one ass at a time.

Q: What's the difference between a doctor and childbirth?

A: One can be terribly painful and sometimes almost unbearable while the other is just having a baby.

Q: What do you do with a cardiovascular surgeon
   who thinks he's God's gift to women?
A: Exchange him.

Q: What is triple antibiotic coverage to an orthopod?
A: *Three* grams of Ancef.

Q: How do you stump an ER doctor?
A: Ask him what the second dose is.

Q: What does a cardiologist do when a patient
   has a heart attack and dies while walking out
   of his office?
A: Turns him around so it looks like the patient is
   walking into his office.

Q: What do you call an 85 year-old pathologist?
A: A mid-career professional.

Q: What is an orthopedic surgeon's definition
   of holistic medicine?
A: Treating the whole bone, not just the fracture.

Q: Why don't psychiatrists go into surgery?
A: Because it's not invasive enough!

Q: What do you call the surgical drape separating the anesthesiologist from the surgeon?
A: The blood-brain barrier.

Q: How do you know if there's a surgeon at your party?
A: He'll tell you.

Q: Why did the neurosurgeon get kicked out of mass at the Vatican?
A: He offered to sign autographs.

Q: How can you tell an anesthesiologist is winking at you?
A: She has one eye open.

Q: What does a neurosurgeon call a handshake?
A: The physical exam.

Q: What is neurology?
A: The 15 minutes of guess work before the CT results come back.

Q: What do you call an intern with an opinion?
A: Wrong.

Q: What do you call a doctor who finished last in his medical school?
A: Doctor.

Q: What's the difference between a smart doctor and a stupid doctor?
A: Nothing. They both think they know everything.

Q: What do you do when you find a dead anesthesiologist in the hallway?
A: Put a cup of coffee next to him so it looks like he died on the job.

Q: How do you confuse an orthopedist?
A: Hand him a stethoscope.

Q: What does it mean when the doctor says you have six months to live?
A: You have five months to pay.

Q: What's the difference between a bullet and a surgeon?
A: The bullet only kills once.

Q. Will dermatologists be any different in the next century?
A. No, and if you call right now, you might get an appointment by then.

Q: What's the difference between an urologist and an anesthesiologist?
A: The urologist plays with someone else's penis during surgery.

Q: What do urologists and anesthesiologists have in common?
A: They both work with dicks.

Seating Arrangements

A philanthropist, a lawyer and a surgeon were in an airplane that crashed. They're up in heaven, and God's sitting on a great throne. God addresses the philanthropist first.

"What do you believe in?"
The philanthropist says, "I believe in helping people less fortunate than myself."
God says "Okay. Come and sit at my left."

God then addresses the lawyer.
"What do you believe in?"
The lawyer says, "I believe in protecting freedom and democracy by working for equal rights and social justice."
God says "Come and sit at my right."

God then addresses the surgeon.
"What do you believe in?"
The surgeon says, "I believe you're in my chair."

Hiding Money from a Doctor

Q: How do you hide a dollar from a general surgeon?
A: Put it in the patient's chart.

Q: How do you hide a dollar from an orthopedic surgeon?
A: Put it in a book.

Q: How do you hide a dollar from a radiologist?
A: Tape it to a patient.

Q: How do you hide a dollar from an internist?
A: Hide it under a dressing.

Q: How do you hide a dollar from a psychiatrist?
A: Anywhere—just call a code blue and they'll head away from it.

Q: How do you hide a dollar from a neurosurgeon?
A: Tape it to his kid's forehead.

Q: How do you hide a dollar from an ob-gyn?
A: Put it anywhere above the patient's waist.

Q: How do you hide a dollar from a plastic surgeon?
A: Put it on a patient who's actually sick.

Q: How do you hide a dollar from a neurologist?
A: It doesn't really matter if they look for it or not; the MRI will see it if it's there.

Q: How do you hide a dollar from an ophthalmologist?
A: Leave it at the hospital over the weekend.

Q: How do you hide a dollar from an anesthesiologist?
A: You can put it basically anywhere in the hospital except on her coffee or *People* magazine.

Q: How do you hide a dollar from an ER doc?
A: You can't. He'll have a dozen consultants looking for it in under 5 minutes.

Q: How do you hide a dollar from a pediatrician?
A: Not necessary. They've forgotten what money looks like.

Q: How do you hide a dollar from a dermatologist?
A: It's a trick question. You can't hide money from a dermatologist.

Doctors and Lightbulbs

Q: How many doctors does it take to change
   a light bulb?
A: That depends on whether it has health insurance.

Q: How many doctors does it take to change
   a light bulb?
A: Screw you. That's a nurse's job.

Q: How many doctors does it take to change
   a light bulb?
A: My God! It burnt out!! Sell all my G.E. stock stat!!!

Q: How many doctors does it take to change
   a light bulb?
A: None. They just tell it to take two aspirin and call
   in the morning.

Q: How many doctors does it take to change a light bulb?

A: One, but he has to have a nurse to tell him which end to screw in.

Q: How many doctors does it take to change a light bulb?

A: Three. One to order a replacement bulb, one to watch a nurse do it, and one to bill it all to Medicare.

Q: How long does it take a doctor to change a light bulb?

A: It depends how long it takes him to find a nurse.

Surgeons and Lightbulbs

Q: How many surgeons does it take to change a light bulb?

A: None. They would wait for a suitable donor and do a filament transplant.

Q: How many orthopedic surgeons does it take to change a light bulb?

A: Two. One to hold the bulb and the other to hammer it in.

Q: How many orthopedic surgeons does it take to change a light bulb?

A: Two. One to assess the bulb's range of motion and one to write "Dark. Cause? Refer medics."

Q: How many cardiothoracic surgeons does it take to change a light bulb?

A: One. He just holds the bulb up to the light fitting and waits for the room to revolve around him.

Q: How many plastic surgeons does it take to change a light bulb?

A: It depends what you want to change it into.

Q: How many plastic surgeons does it take to change a light bulb?

A: Three. One to take it out and two to give you options for a new bulb.

Q: How many neurosurgeons does it take to change a light bulb?

A: Only one, but first he has to rewire the entire building.

Q: How many surgeons does it take to change a light bulb?

A: Only one. They don't like to share the spotlight.

Other Doctor Specialties and Lightbulbs

Q: How many pathologists does it take to change a light bulb?

A: None. They only sign the death certificate and phone the mortuary.

Q: How many radiologists does it take to change a light bulb?

A: What's a light bulb?

Q: How many internal medicine doctors does it take to change a light bulb?

A: Just one but only after 4 hours of rounds to explain why the light bulb needs to be changed.

Q: How many oncologists does it take to change a light bulb?

A: Two. One to change the bulb and one to form a support group.

Q: How many ER doctors does it take to change a light bulb?

A: One. But the bulb will have to spend four hours in the waiting room.

Q: How many dermatologists does it take to change a light bulb?

A: Only one, but she's not available till next year.

Q: How many pediatricians does it take to change a light bulb?

A: None. Pediatricians never change anything— except diapers.

Other Medical Specialties and Lightbulbs

Q: How many psychiatrists does it take to change a light bulb?

A: Just one, but the light bulb has to really want to change.

Q: How many psychiatrists does it take to change a light bulb?

A: Just one, but they need 15 sessions to do it.

Q: How many psychiatrists does it take to change a light bulb?

A: None. They would diagnose depression and prescribe benzodiazepines.

Q: How many psychiatrists does it take to change a light bulb?

A: How many do you think it takes?

Q: How many veterinarians does it take to change a light bulb?

A: Three. One to change the bulb and two more to complain that an MD makes ten times as much for the same procedure.

Q: How many physical therapists does it take to change a light bulb?

A: None. They just give the dead bulb some exercises to do and hope it will be working a bit better the next time they see it.

Q: How many chiropractors does it take to change a light bulb?

A: One, but it takes six visits.

Nurses, Pharmacists and Lightbulbs

Q: How many nurses does it take to change a light bulb?

A: None. They aren't allowed to. They can determine the health of the bulb, record its health in the charts and order a new bulb, but the doctor has to change it.

Q: How many nurses does it take to change a light bulb?

A: None. Nurses aren't scared of the dark.

Q: How long does it take a nurse to change a light bulb?

A: Only one minute, but then it takes her 45 minutes to document it.

Q: How many residents does it take to change
   a light bulb?

A: One, but an ICU nurse has to tell him how
   to do it.

Q: How many pharmacists does it take to change
   a light bulb?

A: Just one, but he has to do it three times a day,
   for ten days.

Q: How many pharmacists does it take to change
   a light bulb?

A: Just one, but he has to wait on hold on the
   phone as the medical assistant tries to get the
   doctor to approve the change from CFC bulbs to
   incandescent bulbs because the Walgreens club
   card doesn't give discounts on CFC bulbs.

Med Students, Interns and Lightbulbs

Q: How many pre-med students does it take to screw in a light bulb?

A: 100. One to change the light bulb and 99 to stand around wondering why they weren't chosen.

Q: How many pre-med students does it take to screw in a light bulb?

A: Five. One to change the bulb and four to pull the ladder out from under him.

Q: How many pre-med students does it take to screw in a light bulb?

A: Will this question be on the final exam?

Q: How many medical students does it take to change a light bulb?

A: Two and a professor to take the credit.

Q: How many first year medical students does it take to change a light bulb?

A: None. That's a second year subject.

Q: How many interns does it take to change a light bulb?

A: One. But it will probably take him three or four tries to get it right.

Q: How many interns does it take to change a light bulb?

A: One, but it takes him three hours and two phone calls to the electrician before he realizes he forgot to turn the switch on.

The Three Lies of
Cardiothoracic Surgeons

I've only slept with my wife.
It was dry when I closed.
Good job anesthesia.

Med School Exam

In the exam for a med school, students were asked to
rearrange the letters N E P I S to form a body part.
Those who formed SPINE are now chiropractors.

The Cemetery

A man and his son were walking through a cemetery.

The boy said, "Do they bury two people in the
same grave?"

The father said, "Why do you ask?"

The boy said, "That gravestone says: 'Here lies
a surgeon and a humble man.'"

Trip to Hell

A surgeon goes to hell. The devil says, "You have a choice between these two doors. I'll let you have a look in each to see where you want to spend the rest of eternity."

The surgeon opens the first door. It's a surgical intensive care unit with 20 patients all going code blue at the same time. The surgeon says, "No way. Not this one."

The surgeon opens the second door. It has medical records with an infinite hallway of d/c summaries to sign. The surgeon says, "No way. Not this one."

Then the surgeon notices a third door. He opens it and there's a surgeon's lounge with a big screen TV, lots of beer and a beautiful nurse at the beck and call of each surgeon. The surgeon says, "This is the door I choose for eternity."

The devil says, "No. It's got to be one of the first two doors."
The surgeon says, "Why?"
The devil says, "Because the third door is nurse's hell."

Survey

Last month, a survey was conducted by the American Medical Association. The only question asked was: "Would you please give your thoughts about communicating with patients about large fees for hard work."

The survey was a huge failure.

- The cardiothoracic surgeons didn't know what "please" meant.

- The orthopedists didn't know what "thoughts" meant.

- The pathologists didn't know what "communicating" meant.

- The pediatricians didn't know what "large fees" meant.

- The anesthesiologists didn't know what "hard work" meant.

Jokes to Make Other Professions Look Bad

The jokes in this section can be switched around to include any professionals you want—bankers, stock brokers, dentists, consultants, engineers or whoever is giving you a hard time. (I've written them with lawyers, doctors and CPAs.) They can stop your headache at its source—the jerk telling lawyer jokes. Use them as needed and take more than two. But *don't* call me in the morning.

The Devil Visit

One night the devil appeared in a CPA's [or doctor's] office. The devil said, "I can increase your income five-fold. Your partners will love you; your clients will respect you; you'll have four months of vacation each year and live to be a hundred. All I require in return is that your wife's soul, your children's souls, and their children's souls rot in hell for eternity."

The CPA [or doctor] thought for a moment and said, "What's the catch?"

The Mars Mission

NASA was interviewing professionals to be sent to Mars. Only one could go—and couldn't return to Earth. The first applicant was a doctor. They asked her how much she wanted to be paid for going. She said, "A million dollars because I want to donate it for the advancement of medical research." The next applicant was a lawyer. He said, "I want $2 million—a million for my family and a million for charity legal work for poor people." The last applicant was a CPA. When asked how much money he wanted, he whispered in the interviewer's ear, "Three million dollars." The interviewer said, "Why so much?" The CPA said, "If you give me $3 million, I'll give you $1 million, I'll keep $1 million, and we'll send the doctor to Mars."

The Bear

A doctor and a CPA walking through the woods spotted a vicious-looking bear.

The doctor immediately opened his briefcase, pulled out a pair of sneakers, and started putting them on.

The CPA looked at him and said, "You're crazy! You can't outrun that bear!"

The doctor said, "I don't have to. I only have to outrun you."

The Empty Seat

A [CPA or doctor] keeps trying to get tickets to a hit Broadway show. Finally, he gets two seats a year in advance. The great night arrives. He goes to the theater. And sits in his seat. A woman in back of the [CPA or doctor] sees that the seat next to him is empty. She asks him why. The [CPA or doctor] says, "My wife couldn't make it." The woman says, "Don't you have friends or relatives who could have used the seat?" The [CPA or doctor] says, "Oh, they're all at her funeral."

The House in Heaven

The Pope and a [CPA or doctor] are at the Pearly Gates. St. Peter shows them to their new lodgings. First they stop at a huge palatial estate with a swimming pool, tennis court and three car garage. St.Peter says, "This is for the [CPA or doctor]." Then St. Peter takes the Pope to a small apartment in a six-story walk-up. The Pope can't believe it. He says to St. Peter, "You put that [CPA or doctor] in that big estate and this is all I get? I was a Pope. I helped millions of people to follow God's commandments." St. Peter said, "We have lots of Popes up here. That other guy was the first [CPA or doctor] who ever made it."

The Right Answer

A corporate executive was interviewing applicants for a job. He asked each person, "How much is two and two?"

The first applicant was a lawyer. He said, "Four."

The second applicant was a doctor. He said "4.00."

The third applicant was a CPA. He said "How much do you want it to be?"

The Brain Store

A guy goes into a brain store to get a brain for an experiment. A sign shows the profession of each brain. But it doesn't show any prices. So he asks,

"How much is a lawyer's brain?
The manager says, "One hundred dollars an ounce."
"How much is an engineer's brain?"

"One hundred fifty dollars an ounce."
"And how much is a [doctor or CPA]'s brain?"
"One thousand dollars an ounce."

So the guy asks, "How come the [doctor or CPA] brain costs so much more?"
The manager says, "Do you know how many [doctors or CPAs] it takes to find an ounce of brain?"

The Liar

Two boys were arguing when a [doctor or CPA] entered the room. The [doctor or CPA] said, "Why are you arguing?" One boy said, "We found a ten dollar bill and decided to give it to whoever tells the biggest lie." The [doctor or CPA] said, "You should be ashamed of yourselves. When I was your age I didn't even know what a lie was." The boys gave the ten dollars to the [doctor or CPA].

The Last Words

A CPA, a doctor and a lawyer were captured by terrorists. The terrorist leader said, "Before we shoot you, you will be allowed last words. Please let me know what you wish to talk about."

The CPA said, "I wish to speak about the beauty of mathematical relationships. How they are a form of art."

The doctor said, "I wish to talk about the nobility of medicine. How our generosity saves lives and makes the world a better place."

The lawyer said, "Just shoot me before the doctor starts talking."

The Brass Rat

A man browsing in a curio shop saw a brass rat. He asked the shopkeeper how much it cost. After a lot of negotiation, they agreed on a price. But the shopkeeper warned, "This sale is final. If you leave with the brass rat, I won't take it back under any circumstances." The man said OK and left with the brass rat. He was walking home when he noticed a live rat come out of an alley and begin to follow him. Soon more rats were following him. He began to trot, then jog, then run. But the rats kept up. After a few minutes, thousands of rats were chasing him. So he ran to the river and threw the brass rat into the water. To his amazement the live rats followed the brass rat and in seconds they had all drowned. The man thought for a moment and then ran back to the curio shop. When the shopkeeper saw him, he shouted, "I told you the sale was final! You can't return the brass rat!" The man said, "Return it? You don't understand. I came back to see if you have any brass CPAs [or doctors]."

The Embezzler

A man who was a courier for the mob also happened to be deaf and mute. When he embezzled $1 million from the mob, the boss found out and sent a hitman to the man's house to collect the stolen funds. The courier's brother, a CPA [or doctor], was also at the house. Because he knew sign language he acted as an interpreter between the courier and the hitman.

Hitman: "Where is the money?"

The courier signs he doesn't know.

CPA [or Dr.]: "He says he doesn't know."

Hitman: "Tell me where the money is or you're a dead man!"

The courier signs fast and furiously that the money is in a safe that is hidden in the floorboard of his closet and gives the combination.

Hitman: "Okay. What did he say?"

CPA [or Dr.]: "He says you don't have the guts to go through with it!"

The Test

A doctor and a lawyer were finalists for an executive position at an insurance company. And they both had good qualifications. To determine which to hire, an HR manager gave them a test. Upon completion of the test, both missed only one of the questions.

The HR manager told the doctor, "Thanks for your interest, but we're giving the job to the lawyer."

The doctor said, "Why? We both got 9 questions correct."

The HR manager said, "We didn't base our decision on the correct answers, but on the question you both missed."

The doctor said, "How can one incorrect answer be better than the other?"

The HR manager said, "Well, on question #5, the lawyer wrote 'I don't know.' You wrote 'Neither do I.'"

The Restroom

A CPA, a doctor and a lawyer were at urinals in a restroom. The CPA finishes and walks over to the sink to wash his hands. Very carefully. He uses paper towel after paper towel and ensures that every single spot of water on his hands is dried. Turning to the other two, he says, "CPAs are trained to be extremely thorough."

The doctor finishes his task at the urinal and he proceeds to wash his hands. He uses a single paper towel and makes sure that he dries his hands using every available portion of the paper towel. He turns and says, "Doctors are not only trained to be extremely thorough but we are also trained to be extremely efficient."

The lawyer finishes and walks straight for the door. "Lawyers don't pee on their hands."

Part III

Jokes That Make Lawyers Look Good

Every joke must have a target. That's the claim you'll hear ad nauseam from all sorts of comedy experts, pundits and practitioners. They insist there always has to be a butt of the joke. And, for the most part, I agree. Certainly, the lawyer jokes that inspired Part I of this book set their sights on ridiculing attorneys. And the jokes in Part II target doctors, CPAs and other professionals.

But my research has shown that it's also possible for a joke to build someone up without tearing anyone down. This type of joke has a subject rather than a target. It makes the subject look good. The point of such a joke is that the subject is smart or honest or creative, some positive trait.

Admittedly, these jokes are rare. Maybe they're just the exceptions that prove the rule. But they do exist.

I've gathered some in this last part of the book. They're jokes that make lawyers look good. You'll notice there aren't a lot of them. Like I said, jokes without targets are rare. But these provide a start. And maybe a potential solution to the age-old problem of negative lawyer jokes.

Here's how.

In the introduction to this book, I wrote about a state bar president in the 1990s who was so frustrated with lawyer jokes that he advised attorneys to tell doctor jokes. Predictably, that approach didn't work. His "solution" only showed that doctors can be rich, greedy and dumb like the lawyers in lawyer jokes. It did nothing to change the underlying public attitude toward lawyers.

That's where jokes that make lawyers look good come in. They emphasize positive traits. I've also included jokes about legal aid lawyers and public interest attorneys. These jokes show that many lawyers are *not* rich and greedy. They sacrifice wealth so they can dedicate their lives to public service.

If lawyers tell and spread the jokes from this part of the book, it's possible that public attitudes will move in a positive direction. Just the possibility is a good start!

It's like water flowing against a boulder. The boulder will eventually become a pebble, but it won't happen overnight.

So sprinkle these jokes throughout your conversations. If you can tap into a well of them, do so and spread the word. It just might make people think of Abraham Lincoln, Mahatma Gandhi and Nelson Mandela when they hear the word "lawyer"—instead of the lawyers in lawyer jokes.

Q: How many lawyers does it take to change
   a light bulb?
A: None, if the lawyers are Abraham Lincoln,
   Mahatma Gandhi or Nelson Mandela. Then
   the light comes from within.

Q: How do you know when someone is about to
   say something smart?
A: When they start with "A lawyer once told me…"

Q: What's the plural of lawyer?
A: Justice.

Q: Why do public service lawyers like the band U2?
A: They're pro Bono.

Q: What do pro bono lawyers charge that poor
   people have and rich people need?
A: Nothing.

Q: How many public service lawyers does it take
   to change a light bulb?
A: One, but she has 172 other light bulbs to
   change first.

Q: How many public interest lawyers does it take to change a light bulb?

A: Two. One to change the bulb and one to shine it on corruption.

Q: What's the definition of an optimist?

A: A public interest lawyer with a mortgage.

Q: What do you call a public interest lawyer in a country club?

A: A visitor.

Q: What's the favorite dog breed of a public service lawyer?

A: The underdog.

Q: How many public interest lawyers does it take to change a light bulb?

A: 100. One to change the bulb and 99 to ensure the power is sold at a fair price.

Q: Did you hear about the legal aid lawyer who made a fortune?

A: Me neither.

The Spouse

A woman had been married eight times, but
her marriages were never consummated. She
explained why.

My first husband was a real estate attorney.
But he couldn't do the deed.

My second husband was an immigration attorney.
He didn't want to cross the border.

My third husband was an environmental attorney.
He didn't like my natural resources.

My fourth husband was a class action attorney.
He only wanted to do it in a group.

My fifth husband was a social security attorney.
He said I wasn't eligible for his benefits.

My sixth husband was a mediation attorney.
He just wanted to talk about it.

My seventh husband was an OSHA attorney.
All he would do is inspect it.

My eighth husband was a trusts and estates attorney.
He didn't like my assets.

Moral: You'll never be screwed by a lawyer.

The Stick-Up

Did you hear about the mugger who stuck up a public interest lawyer?

The mugger said, "Your money or your life."

The lawyer said, "Sorry, I'm a public interest lawyer. I don't have either."

The Wish

A CPA (or doctor or other professional) rubs a lamp and a genie appears.

The genie says, "You get three wishes."

The CPA says, "I'd like to be hundred times smarter."

The genie says, "Done! You're a hundred times smarter. What's your second wish?"

The CPA says, "This is great. Now I want to be a thousand times smarter."

The genie says, "Done! You're a thousand times smarter. What's your last wish?"

The CPA says, "Make me a million times smarter." So the genie turns him into a lawyer.

The Diagnosis

A woman complained to a friend about her physical and mental problems. She couldn't afford a doctor and didn't know what was wrong with her. The friend had a computer program that could diagnose medical conditions. So the friend asked for her symptoms.

The woman said, "I have this nervous twitch in my eyelids and hands."

The friend put it in the computer.

The woman said, "I can only sleep a couple of hours a night."

The friend put it in.

The woman said, "I have a recurring dream that I work on an assembly line that never stops."

The friend put it in.

The woman said, "I have difficulty believing what people tell me."

The friend put it in.

The woman said, "I have a phobia that I'll die in poverty."

The friend said, "Any more symptoms?"

The woman said, "I think that's it."

The friend clicked on "diagnosis" and the hard drive whirred. A few seconds later the diagnosis appeared. It said, "You're a public interest lawyer."

The Idea

There are three convenience stores right next to each other on the main street in town. Each store has one big investor—a CPA, a doctor and a lawyer. One day the store on the left, the CPA's store, put up a big sign: "Sale–Lowest Prices in Town."

The store on the right, the doctor's store, saw this and put up its own sign: "Sale–Rock Bottom Prices."

The store in the middle, the lawyer's store, was very upset.

Then the lawyer got an idea. He hung up a banner. It said "Main Entrance."

Q: What's the difference between a legal aid lawyer and a picnic table?

A: A picnic table can support a family of four.

Q: What do you call a guy who hangs around a bunch of legal aid lawyers?

A: A debt collector.

Q: What's the difference between a well-paid legal aid lawyer and the Invisible Man?

A: You've got more chance of seeing the Invisible Man.

Q: What's the difference between a legal aid lawyer's jokes and his salary?

A: No one ever laughs at his jokes.

Q: What did the legal aid lawyer fill in for "Salary Expected" on a job application?

A: Yes.

Q: What are McDonald's employees now asking public interest lawyers?

A: Can you afford fries with that?

The Eulogy

A CPA, a doctor and a lawyer die in a car accident. They all go to heaven. And they're asked, "When you're in your casket and your friends and family are mourning, what would you like to hear them say about you?

The CPA says, "I would like to hear them say that I was a great CPA of my time, and a great family man."

The doctor says, "I would like to hear that I was a wonderful doctor who made a huge difference in people's lives."

The lawyer says, "I would like to hear them say 'Look, he's moving!'"

Acknowledgments

Many people were instrumental in the creation of this book. Dr. Christine Griger provided her usual extraordinary editing. Susan Leonard provided impeccable design. And Bob Reed provided his publishing know-how.

Special thanks goes to Professor Marsha Cohen of University of California, Hastings College of the Law for sifting through an endless deluge of jokes and comebacks to determine which were worthy of inclusion.

Other friends who suffered through early versions of the book and made useful suggestions include Lu Haussler, Kathy Welton, Elizabeth Symonds, Donna Bedford, Patty White, Sheila Jarret, Loyd Auerbach, Cleone Lyvonne Reed, Melinda Cooper and Julie Horst.

Important help and advice also came from Heather Tamarkin, Norman Mitgang, Sam Kushner, Rachael Brune and Rich Herzfeld.

Many thanks also to Professor Alan Dershowitz and Donna Bedford for their kind words about the book.

I salute you all.

Who Wrote What

Many of the jokes used in this book were found on the Internet. Like folklore, they're familiar to all of us but their authors are unknown. To the best of my knowledge, they fall under the fair use or public domain guidelines of copyright law in the United States.

The introductions to the book and each of its three sections were written by me.

The lawyer jokes in Part I were found on the Internet. The alternative punchlines for them were written by me with one exception. The alternative punchline to "What's the difference between a lawyer and a mosquito?" ("A lawyer has never given anyone malaria.") was written by Bob Mills and first appeared in *The Ultimate Lawyer Quote Book* (2014) published by the American Bar Association. Also first appearing in *The Ultimate Lawyer Quote Book* was "What's the difference between a lawyer and a jellyfish?" ("Aquariums don't beg jellyfish to be on their board of directors.")

The jokes about professionals in Part II were found on the Internet. Some were rewritten slightly by me.

Most of the Q&A jokes in Part III were written by me. A couple were found on the Internet and switched by me. The longer jokes in this section were also found on the Internet and switched by me.

If you identify any material that has not been correctly credited please let me know.

About the Author

Malcolm Kushner, "America's Favorite Humor Consultant," is an internationally acclaimed expert on humor and communication. Since 1982, he has trained thousands of managers, executives and professionals on how to gain a competitive edge with humor. His clients include Aetna, AT&T, Bank of America, American Bar Association, American Medical Association, Defense Research Institute and the IRS.

He is the author of *The Light Touch: How to Use Humor for Business Success*, *Public Speaking For Dummies*, *Vintage Humor For Wine Lovers* and *The Official Book of Mob Humor*, as well as the editor of *The Little Book of Humorous Quotes*. He is also the co-creator of a humor exhibit that appeared at the Ronald Reagan Presidential Library.

Kushner has been profiled in *Time Magazine*, *USA Today*, *The New York Times* and *The Washington Post*. His television and radio appearances include CNN, C-SPAN, "Fox & Friends," National Public Radio, CNBC, "Voice of America" and "The Larry King Show." The Wall Street Journal has called him irrepressible.

Kushner holds an MA in Communications from the University of Southern California and a JD from the University of California, Hastings College of the Law. He has served as a staff attorney for the California Workers' Compensation Appeals Board and practiced law with a major San Francisco firm.

A popular speaker at corporate and association meetings, Kushner has keynoted everywhere from the Smithsonian Institution to the Inc. 500 Conference. He is based in Sacramento, California.

Visit his websites at:
www.kushnergroup.com
www.museumofhumor.com

He can be reached at mk@kushnergroup.com

Made in the USA
Monee, IL
03 December 2019

17873684R00108